A WOMEN'S GUIDE TO SACRED ACTIVISM:
HOW DO WE MOVE FORWARD?

Co-Founder of the global sisterhood of Gather the Women, Marilyn Nyborg brings women's ways of knowing to sacred activism. Hallelujah!

With polish and panache, she gives us keys to the remaking of ourselves, so that we can remake the world. To read this book is to move beyond outmoded and destructive thinking and actions to a new level of empowerment and intelligence, a passion for the possible and the guidance to help make a world that works for all.

Above all, it is to enter into daily life as spiritual exercise, and thereby bring from the Source of existence, the inspiration and genius to guide our lives as spiritual activists. In this, we come to engage the strength of women to "Redeem the time. Redeem the unread vision in the higher dream." T.S. Eliot

Jean Houston, Ph.D, Author, scholar, philosopher and researcher in Human Capacities, is one of the foremost visionary thinkers and doers of our time.

A Women's Guide to Sacred Activism is timely, accessible and resonant. Sharing one woman's journey into purposeful and heart-inspired action, it articulates pathways for sacred activism that are much needed today.

Leading always from the Heart, Ms. Nyborg offers clear guidance for clarifying women's unique calling, and doing the secular yet deeply spiritual work to get out of our own way, and show up differently. With clarity, purpose, intention and power, women can and are leading the way toward the new world we know is possible. This book offers valuable guidance along the way, and is an easy and joyful read.

Nina Simons, cofounder Bioneers, editor Moonrise: The Power of Women Leading from the Heart

A WOMEN'S GUIDE TO SACRED ACTIVISM:
HOW DO WE MOVE FORWARD?

Marilyn Rosenbrock Nyborg

with Marilyn Chambliss and Sushila Mertens

A WOMEN'S GUIDE TO SACRED ACTIVISM:
HOW DO WE MOVE FORWARD?

iUniverse books may be ordered through booksellers or by contacting:

iUniverse
1663 Liberty Drive
Bloomington, IN 47403
www.iuniverse.com
1-800-Authors (1-800-288-4677)

ISBN: 978-1-5320-3044-4 (sc)
ISBN: 978-1-5320-3043-7 (e)

Library of Congress Control Number: 2017912498

Print information available on the last page.

iUniverse rev. date: 11/06/2017

CONTENTS

SIDEBARS

POETRY/ART

SELF REFLECTION

FOREWORD

Marilyn Nyborg is the author of this book. I, Marilyn Chambliss, have helped her design it, but her book grows directly out of her own lived thoughts and experiences. Sushila Mertens describes in her Foreword the special thinking and experiences she has shared with Marilyn creating profound changes in Sushila's own thoughts and actions and leading to their becoming soul sisters. My role has been quite different. Marilyn asked me to help her respond to suggestions her editor had made to an earlier draft. I am the co-author of three published books myself. I am now retired, but as an associate University professor, I studied the characteristics of writing that guide readers to understand and apply what they have read. Working with advanced doctoral students as they crafted their dissertations, I learned how to assist authors to create book length writing that communicates clearly the author's ideas to readers. My goal with this book was to apply what I know about good writing to work with Marilyn to design a book that would be clear and that would help readers apply her ideas to their own lives. Sushila brought her expertise in writing to provide excellent editorial skills. I believe the three of us reached my goal. Folk who have read the almost-ready-to-publish draft have responded very positively and have encouraged Marilyn to get it published so that they can put it to good use. I am very proud of our work! But it hasn't been easy. And working on this book has changed me profoundly in ways I never could have imagined.

Good reading is hard writing, Maya Anjelou has explained. When Marilyn shared the early draft with me, I struggled unsuccessfully to identify the main points--the themes--of the book. And I kept asking, "Where did these lists of suggestions come from?" My own background differed so from Marilyn's that I could not fill in any missing pieces, and I was quite confused. I thought, "Can I help? Where would we begin?" When I shared my reactions with Marilyn, she seemed discouraged. So, I decided to try, and started asking her questions. "When did this start?" "Why?" "What did you conclude?" "And then what happened?" As the three of us worked together to the end, I often found myself asking questions. The answers fascinated me! Together we identified a pattern that was exemplified again and again in Marilyn's thinking and resulting actions. A very clear theme appeared, a theme that I think you, the reader, will find very helpful in creating your own Sacred Activism.

I have learned when working with an author to recraft writing, it is important to be sure to maintain the author's thinking, style, and individual words unless something needs to be clarified. So, although my influence is quite extensive, I am not the author. Marilyn is indeed the author with Sushila's lovely editorial help. My goal always has been to support Marilyn to design her own work so that it communicates clearly. And working with her on this wonderful book has changed me profoundly as I've already suggested. Next I describe that change. Regardless of your history, even if it is as different from Marilyn's as mine, I'd like to reassure you of the effect you can expect.

Most of my life, I would have been bothered by the

title and probably would have avoided the book. I would have decided before reading the first word that I was not interested either in being "sacred" or an "activist." How I have changed! My discomfort with anything sacred grew out of my highly religious childhood. Wonderful, kind, and "liberal" as my parents were, placing religion at the center of life made no sense to me. I was a humanist, kind and ethical to be sure, but accepting reality as the material world that I could touch, see, smell, hear, and taste, a world that I could use science to understand. But then a woman who was very dear to me died, and I began to have experiences that I could only describe as her reaching out to me to communicate. I started to meditate, practice yoga, read books with sacred themes, and attend a wonderful church that openly accepted my unconventional spiritual experiences and beliefs. I had become drawn to the sacred.

My discomfort with activism also developed from early experiences. A young woman in the 1960's and 1970's living both in New York City and the San Francisco Bay Area, I watched activists from the sidelines, never actually participating. I was deeply concerned with the violence, the destruction of property, and the breaking of traditional norms that I often saw and chose instead to lead a conventional life. I married, raised two daughters, and peacefully attended school eventually earning my PhD, while remaining politically liberal and supporting both civil rights and anti-war movements. But I always was careful not to ruffle any feathers.

As you will see from reading about Marilyn's wonderful life, wedding the sacred with activism fits me today very well. How I loved her answers to my questions, descriptions of her thinking and her actions through the years up to today, and her very thoughtful recommendations. I am becoming a Sacred Activist, asking and answering the questions she raises. What do I care about deeply? What is the source of my motivation? How could I take leadership? What actions would build on my particular strengths? I have joined groups of like-minded people. I am learning how to listen to people who have different views and search for common ground. I have identified two issues that I care about deeply and am gathering as much information as I can (one of my strengths). I plan to use my writing both to communicate and become a leader by publishing in as many major newspapers as I can. I'm well on the road to creating a life that shares far more in common with Marilyn Nyborg than my first name. And I'm excited!

Marilyn Chambliss

Marilyn Nyborg is a visionary who changed my life. I, Sushila Mertens, first saw Marilyn on stage at a Gather the Women Nevada County (GTWNC) International Women's Day event. I remember thinking "I want to work with her." I eventually volunteered for GTWNC and sat in circle with Marilyn and the other women on the leadership Steering Wheel. After getting to know me, Marilyn asked if I would help her edit her newsletter, *Through Women's Eyes*. I said, "Yes" and it was the first of many to Marilyn's requests for me to stretch beyond my comfort level and blossom.

Marilyn was always opening to new experiences and exploring other groups and seminars that were returning to our relationship with the earth, the divine feminine and our purpose of empowering women to take actions at every level of leadership. Together we traveled to Los Angeles, New Mexico, Seattle, and San Francisco. I was overjoyed to know we were not alone in wanting to co-create a world that honors life and gives the feminine an equal voice at all tables.

I was also blessed to grow from assistant to soul sister with Marilyn as we integrated each experience. Being raised in a modest middle-class family, my experiences had been limited by unconscious beliefs around money, worth, and the meaning of power. Marilyn's insights into personality and life guided me to let go of limiting beliefs and step into the possible.

I am always in awe of Marilyn's insights and life experiences. When an idea enters her awareness, she creates the actions needed to bring the idea to form. Marilyn suggested we create a question guide for the DVD *The Book of Jane* that she produced. We did not realize that the guide would grow into her book. Her first attempt to expand the guide was sent back from her editor with suggestions. Not to be stopped, Marilyn asked Marilyn Chambliss and me to help her. Working on the writing process led me to deepen my understanding of Marilyn's life experiences and how she takes responsibility to create what she craves in her world. Marilyn's story gives us clues on how to be in the world as a co-creator rather than a victim or a helpless observer. In the process of writing this book I watched Marilyn clarify why and how she became the woman she is. Her life has affected not only my life but countless others. Marilyn has demonstrated a life and means of being a Sacred Activist.

Since meeting Marilyn, I realized women will not be represented unless they step up and lead. My first political activism was volunteering with a local woman's campaign for Congress. I needed to learn how government works and how to overcome the challenges. Sometimes I accompanied her to campaign events, but mostly I made phone calls and stamped thank you letters. To step up and support her, I joined the Democratic Women's Club and became an officer and then president for two years and liaison to the Democratic Central Committee (DCC), eventually becoming a DCC member and Chair of the Candidate Recruitment and Support committee.

I also applied to be on the County Public Cemetery Board and was reappointed for my 2nd term. Due to my persistence and belief in natural end of life alternatives, our Board created and passed the first Green Burial policies in the Public Cemeteries of California. My involvement in local politics has expanded through Indivisible Women that Marilyn co-created.

Through Indivisible Women, Marilyn initiated Reaching Across the Aisle with Living Room Conversations. LRC's promote conversation ground rules that Marilyn follows in her life and in this book. Having been mentored by Marilyn over the years, her words have affected my relationships. In the past, I would avoid speaking with people opposed to my viewpoints. One day at the Democrats County Fair booth, I talked with a man for 30 minutes, asking him questions about his viewpoints and he asking me questions about my views. There was respect and curiosity. There was no need to be right or win. After the conversation, the other women in the booth told me they were amazed that I was able to talk to this particular man for so long and not be upset. My personal work had helped me remain calm and listen, and ask questions to understand and connect. I called Marilyn to share how profoundly different this experience was from the usual political encounter. I was viscerally feeling what I had called Sacred Activism.

I am grateful for Marilyn's commitment to complete this book and share her journey and wisdom with you. We hope you apply this book to your life and you connect with what moves you.

Be vigilant in your awareness of your motivations, your thoughts and your actions. My wish is that you too realize you are living Sacred Activism.

Sushila Mertens

ACKNOWLEDGMENTS

I am very grateful to all the people included in this book for who they are, for what they contribute in the world, and for the inspiration I received for my sacred activism. They are our models and way-showers.

Special hugs and thanks to Dr. Marilyn Chambliss for her insights and interviews, her writing and editing skills, organizing my ideas and words into a readable book, and her professional expertise in publishing. I am deeply grateful.

Heartfelt thanks to Sushila Mertens for our many levels of traveling together these last seven years, her writing and editing skills, and her demonstrating everything written here. I value her encouragement that this book would bring more women to understanding and living Sacred Activism.

Special acknowledgement and appreciation to Jane Evershed and Shiloh Sophia McCloud for allowing me to include their heart opening poetry and art. My acknowledgement and appreciation also to good friend and artist extraordinaire Barbara Bitner who took Marilyn Chambliss's ideas and designed a wonderful graphic to guide a reader's path in becoming a sacred activist. This book would not be complete without their visionary creativity, which is an essential component in transformation.

Thank you to Andrew Harvey for his work and allowing me to quote his words on Sacred Activism from his website; to Nina Simons and Jean Houston for their life work and testimonies; to the founders and participants in the Creative Initiative Foundation that opened me to a deeper purpose for living; and to all the readers of the manuscript that provided support and contributed insights.

To Georgia Dow, touchstone for my life, my partner in life of 36 years for an exciting adventure.

And to our friend and spiritual companion, Tantra Maat, for her support and encouragement

I apologize for any names I failed to mention or errors or omissions in acknowledging any words I heard and did not note your name. I would be grateful to be notified of any corrections that should be incorporated in the next edition or reprint of this book.

Marilyn Rosenbrock Nyborg

WHY READ?

This book is easy to read and even easier to follow, or so I think. However, in the off chance that I am mistaken, I have included road maps of sorts throughout to guide you by foreshadowing what is to come. The book is multi-layered. It is intended first to support you to do your personal work. We must begin with our inner world, connecting with the source of our highest self. Next we understand how we see our world from family patterns and conditioning. We deal with our anger, frustration and hate before engaging with the anger, frustration and violence of the world we seek to change. In other words, we must get clear, or we will take our anger and frustrations into our work and project them on those who oppose our opinion, creating more separation and anger. For example, if you are upset with war (aren't we all?) it does not help to be pissed for peace. It is matching the energy of that which you seek to change with the same energy, the energy of war. Fighting war with war has never worked. You are encouraged to come into a level of awareness where your motivation for a positive future does not recreate the paradigms you seek to change.

The second part of this book is to lead you through choices you can make to become a Sacred Activist. Bring your love and your vision to those you hold as opposition and enemies. Reflection pages will guide you through self-reflection and an understanding of your motivations. Evaluate your passions, interest and willingness to make a difference. Are you willing to speak out when it is not popular to do so? How confident are you? How courageous?

The third intention is encouragement to take action. Work with the resources and ideas of how to create action with a willingness to speak up and speak out in loving ways. Should you collaborate with established groups or create a new group to bring about positive change? What already exists and does it align with your passion? What is duplicable? How much time and energy will you commit? Does your sacred activism remediate the issue that undergirds all other issues--climate change?

It is our hope that this book will inspire you, encourage you, create ideas for your own activism and motivate you to pass this book on! It appears that the world needs us; Sacred Activism as we envision it must be led by women.

When women rise....ALL humanity is lifted.

HOW THIS GUIDE CAME INTO BEING

I thought I had completed this book. I believed I'd covered the how, what, why, and when a woman would need to move forward into Sacred Activism. Among those who read the manuscript, the responses were positive. But one of my readers, Marilyn Chambliss, was concerned. "You are missing from the book," she explained. "Perhaps your story would trigger in your readers their own participation and give them a new perspective on what may appear at first to be obstacles." She asked me how, what, why, and when questions to guide my thinking about my own experiences. For example:

- When did your journey toward Sacred Activism start?
- How did you become a Sacred Activist?
- What happened?
- How did your experiences lead to your understanding of Sacred Activism and your recommendations for women who wished to become a Sacred Activist?

In answering these questions, I began to walk down memory lane. Soon I was writing a long bio. My intention has been to offer my experiences, my motivations for what I have done, and the skills I have developed. Important to me has been, through the story of my own life, to support the reader along her own path.

While I may not know directly all of the people and issues I have impacted, I have changed the world around me, initiating events, bringing people together, developing programs and presentations, and forwarding my beliefs and ideals. More and more, I have expressed genuine interest in and curiosity about the people I meet, seeing in them who they are and their potential. A wonderful outcome for me is that I have fine-tuned my own Soul and deepened my understanding of life and purpose. I have become a Sacred Activist.

Women often say they are not ready to be public with what they believe. They want to hold back until they are ready, if ever. I know no other way to "get ready" than to jump in and do it. Confidence is built this way. Men do tend to do just that; jump in and learn as they go. That's what I did.

What makes women's Sacred Activism different from

activism? This is the question I kept asking myself. My motivations to create change went deeper than *The Free Dictionary* definition of activism: "The use of direct, often confrontational action, such as a demonstration or strike, in opposition to or support of a cause."

My actions came from an inner longing for connection and community. An openness to understand fed my desire to dialogue with both those sharing my experiences and those unaware of my experiences or I theirs. Through my "activism" I always found mentors, peers, and organizations who connected me to the information or place I needed to act with and from.

My involvement in the Civil Rights and the Creative Initiative Movements during the 60's and 70's were steps of self-exploration and empowerment. Although I held no formal degrees or titles, I never hesitated to call a speaker or author, introduce myself, and ask questions. Through the years my life has been blessed with knowing many conscious leaders, writers, and movers and shakers who have been an inspiration.

I noticed a common theme of nonviolence and respect for life in the actions of the most effective women activists including Leymah Gbowee, a Liberian activist who led a women's peace movement that helped bring an end to her country's long civil war, a story depicted in *Pray the Devil Back to Hell*. Wangari Muta Maathai was a Kenyan environmental and political activist. In 1977 she founded the Green Belt Movement, an environmental non-governmental organization focused on the planting of trees, environmental conservation, and women's rights. Helen Mary Caldicott is an Australian physician, author, and anti-nuclear advocate who has founded several associations dedicated to opposing the use of nuclear power, depleted uranium munitions, nuclear weapons and their proliferation, war and military action in general, and a friend of Creative Initiative leadership. These three women were models for living their deepest spiritual visions in their actions that transformed existing political, economic, and social conditions.

Andrew Harvey introduced me to the term *sacred activism* that aptly described how I wanted to live my life. He emphasized acting from "profound spiritual and psychological self-awareness rooted in divine truth, wisdom, and compassion." The source of motivation for action is very significant for both the doer and the outcome. Acting from love or unconscious anger could have very different results.

Reading Harvey and other life-enhancing activists led me to explore my life and what motivated my own actions. My self-reflection confirmed that my social actions have always come from an inner need for solutions and reconciliation. If I needed help for my new role as parent, I would create a support system. If I saw injustice, I would ask what am I to do to bring justice? What group could teach me to educate people about equality and peace? How can I motivate women to find their voices and speak for what is needed?

My inward search for solutions was like a guiding compass. This compass led me to just the right people, places, and events that were part of the actions I needed to take for my growth, as well as toward the future I wanted to be part of.

Sacred Activism is a way of life that does not justify the means to the end. It is essential to know yourself and your motivations. It is a lifelong occupation to be present to both your inner and outer world.

I kept returning to the question, "What am I feeling and doing that is not described by Sacred Activism? What is missing from the discussions of Sacred Activism?" I was not hearing the nuances of how I feel, think, and act. What made my experience different?

The idea to write a book about women's Sacred Activism developed from the short film I had created from *The Book of Jane* by Jane Evershed. After reading the book I called Jane, introduced myself, and said, "Jane, you wrote my book!" After rereading it over and over I called her again and told her I could see it being made into a very powerful film. Jane agreed to narrate the film and worked with me on the project. I promoted the film as a catalyst for positive change and why we needed to imagine the world we would like to see if women were co-leading it. I showed the film to groups and asked the women provocative questions to take the audience from passive listening to questioning our history and our beliefs, and to inspire thoughts about women co-creating a sustainable world. I developed these questions into *The Book of Jane* discussion guide.

It was through refining the discussion guide into this book that I deeply explored the experience of my Sacred Activism. Sacred Activism comes from the deep connection to the inner life. We all have an inner world that is quite distinct from the outer world we encounter with our physical senses. It is the world we meet when we have an emotional reaction, an idea, or close our eyes and live in our fantasies, imagination or dreams. Women's Sacred Activism comes from a connection of this inner world to the internal Divine

Feminine. This connection creates a natural receptive opening to the Divine combined with the powerful physical grounding to the earth, an energetic life-giving union of the Creator and physical. We become aware that the Divine is one with all of life.

Oneness is a radically different social concept from a world that seeks to conquer and divide people from people, people from nature, rich from poor. Females around the world are still excluded from going to school, from equal rights, from equal sexual standards, from equal pay. Privileged men as entitled citizens do not voluntarily share their privileges with women. I believe most privileged men remain unconscious of their entitlement and the issues women still face in their daily lives, which are perpetuated by these men without ever directly affecting them.

It will take women to wake up and to envision what an equal world would look like. What would women do differently if:

- They could both parent and share their greatest gifts with the world?
- They knew they could take time off for their children's development and not lose pay or advancement in their careers?
- They knew their ideas and voices would make policies that support families, life, and the planet?
- They knew they could go anywhere on a campus, a military mission, a park or street and not be afraid of being raped?
- They felt safety was never an issue?

- They could both broaden and deepen our language, whose origin is based on male experiences, by bringing in the experiences of women and girls?

How can women change the current paradigm of a world that focuses on war, terrorism, guns, death, and profit, and take a stand against everything from germs, cancer, and climate change, to terrorism?

Something happened January 21, 2017. Millions of women marched in Washington D.C. and across the country in sisterhood and common goals. Women joined us internationally as well. Watching or participating in that worldwide demonstration for a government that honors all people including women and children, people can no longer ignore the levels of societal influence being brought to bear.

Following this rising up and standing for life, people who never considered politics to be interesting and important came forward to join with the women who have been activists. They learned who their representatives were by name and the stands they hold. They became educated on the issues that we face as a country. They learned where money is being spent and where it is not. People everywhere demanded that their representative hold public town hall meetings. And where representatives did hold town halls, the turnout has been overwhelming. The questions asked are fact based and intense.

Politics is about influence. When asked what women want, I would answer, to share power and have an equal voice. We ask of men to listen, don't interrupt, and don't claim our ideas as your own. Stand behind us. Stand next to us. It's our turn to lead and to influence outcome.

We stop fighting. We envision. We create. We come from love. We gain strength by learning to trust and support each other. We unite as women and the men who love us. We come from fullness, and we share. We come from solutions in which we take responsibility, and we implement. We step from being powerless to speaking with confidence and power. We are persistent until we are heard. This book is about growing and adapting a new model of womanhood that includes activism and empowerment.

It is my hope that my story and the suggestions I provide will guide you into self-reflection and an understanding of your motivations for activism, and then inspire you to take action.

MY STORY OF BECOMING A SACRED ACTIVIST

Life's Train Wrecks Can Point You To Where You Need To Go

November 5th, 1956. It took a train wreck to interrupt my life plans and send me towards a different life. I was on my way home from DePaul University and settled into my seat on the "L" train when it crashed into the Milwaukee Limited preparing to leave the Wilson station in Chicago. The impact threw me forward, fracturing my neck, smashing my nose and giving me a concussion. After weeks in the hospital, and surgery repaired my crushed nose and septum, I began to have headaches that were so severe I could not continue my formal education.

My options were limited by my circumstances, so I did what most women did in the 50's and 60's. First I found a job as a typist, and then I married a man - with a degree from Northwestern University. We soon moved to California, far away from my mother and grandmother, who had raised me.

Like many other Californians, we were transplants without family and old friends for support and connection when our first son was born. I was the only child of an only child. I knew nothing about babies. There were no personal computers or Google to answer questions in the 60's. I developed my capacity to research, to reach out and connect. Circumstances can be highly motivating! I figured I was not the only mother who needed help, so I initiated a group called Parents At Large. I brought together new mothers, and with information from my birthing instructor, invited doctors, educators and other speakers to discuss parenting. I rented places to meet. This was the first time I had organized. I was motivated by necessity. I also discovered that my gift of reaching out to others and making connections brought forth good results.

Without formal education and theories, I was developing my inner senses and a desire to contribute. Looking back, I now appreciate how my life situations allowed me time for deep thinking and questioning.

I was raised in a racist home. My earlier years growing up in Baltimore and Atlanta exposed me to the ugly sounds of racism. I accepted the superiority of white skin. It took many years before I saw the richness of diversity. I did not want to be like my mother in many ways. I paid attention to the civil rights movement, and through my later work, I thought I would rather be black. I felt the white culture was led by patriarchal intellect. I felt the flow of the feminine in the fluidity and expressiveness of the black community.

When I heard about a black child who was mistreated in school, I learned that the black parents had rallied and called for more sensitivity and inclusion of black history. I found myself in a meeting in East Palo Alto, a very poor black section of the Bay Area peninsula. I was one of two white faces present. Gertrude, who eventually became the mayor, asked me, "Why are you here?" and I replied, "How can I help?" She strongly told me, "Go home to your own community. That's where the problem is and work is needed." Without taking offense I got it that the lack of understanding of racial inequality needed attention in my own neighborhood.

I wondered what actions I could begin in my own

community to build bridges. Retrospectively I realized I had developed my emotional intelligence, a gift that is not nurtured in our culture. Emotional intelligence, defined in Wikipedia, is the ability of individuals to recognize their own, and other people's emotions, to recognize and label different feelings, to guide thinking and behavior using emotional information, and to change environments or achieve goals by managing and/or adjusting emotions. I wanted to change how people interacted. I wanted to build understanding and respect between people. Again I reached out with a shared desire for change and peace. I began working with the YWCA where we created home visit exchanges. We arranged for black and white families to go to each other's homes and see the human sameness of our families. We had dialogue about our lives. "What was the black perspective on the problems we faced?" "Did the white families identify or experience the same challenges?" I noted that the civil rights movement and the growing feminist movement both were up against the white masculine status quo. My brain was creating connections and leading me to feminist activism.

I so valued the action of talking together for creating solutions; I stepped into leadership on the Y Board. Our face to face communication seems so archaic now in the 21st Century; however, I wonder if we need interpersonal communication skills now more than ever as technology reaches more people who are not critically evaluating information or listening to understand. We began living in a world of data, without personal interaction and experience.

In my leadership, I met a black social worker from Stanford and asked him to create an encounter group, a model developed in the '60's in which *a* group of people met to increase self-awareness and social sensitivity. Sometimes it is called sensitivity training. My role was to set up the space and find people to attend. I called on city council members, ministers, and other community leaders to come together with black members of the community. We asked the deepest questions. "How does it feel to be black?" "What is the white perspective on the civil rights movement?" "How do you respond to a different perspective?" Together we processed, cried, got angry and worked together in the community to bring understanding, change and build relationships.

The reality of discrimination in housing led me to become the Director of Fair Housing in Palo Alto for three years. The civil rights act signed into law in April 1968, popularly known as the Fair Housing Act, prohibited discrimination concerning the sale, rental and financing of housing based on race, religion, national origin and sex.

The head of our board was Jing Lyman, wife of Stanford's president Richard Lyman. Jing was an amazing example of feminine power long before we used the term. We had access to many of Stanford's resources. A student joined us to create the first audit of housing discrimination by sending a qualified black person to apply for a rental followed by a white person with a similar resume. Quite often the black applicant would find the rental already taken; within hours the white applicant found it available. I ran that project and presented recommendations for taking corrective actions to various city councils.

I encountered many people throughout the years who did not agree with me. It did not stop me from creating relationship. I tend to share what I believe in. If a person cannot relate to one concept, I take another path. I am not looking to defend or convince anyone to agree with me. I am genuinely interested in how others think and believe and how they got there. I find it fascinating to ask questions about their belief systems. I never back off of these conversations unless it is evident the person may be violent or irrational and cannot engage in the exchange. The non-threatening openness leads to fascinating explorations and deeper relationships.

Choosing New Beliefs

My parents divorced when I was nine. My mother and I moved from a life with nannies and maids to a very small, smoke filled apartment with my grandmother in Chicago. It was made very clear to me that only white, Republican, Lutheran, and preferably Swedish people were acceptable. The rules did not necessarily apply to my mother who dated outside the box. My mother was also depressed and an alcoholic. She was once absent for a year in my life, and then I began to mother my mother.

What I have noticed is that people either strive to become like their parents and to be accepted by the family, or they reject the model their parents live. I rejected my mother's beliefs and investigated other ideologies. My best friend in high school was Catholic, and introduced me to Mass where I loved the ritual and incense but still felt loyal to my Lutheran indoctrination. Working part time at Stouffer's Restaurant, I was adopted by my Irish co-workers who took me to their dances and St. Peters. I was soon going to church at lunch or after work. I feasted on stories about the saints and conversions. When I turned 18, I made a choice to be baptized Catholic and attend a Catholic university. This was not the plan my mother and grandmother had in mind for me.

After the train wreck and my migraines, I had to leave the tension in our apartment and find a job to support myself. I was hired as a typist for the National Congress of Parents and Teachers, currently known as the Parent Teacher Association (PTA). This organization was all female at that time, including the administrators. These women were my first positive role models of strong compassionate women who believed they could make a difference. I did not yet see myself in a leadership role.

Most of my friends were married, and I was beginning to feel I would never find the right one. I soon met my husband to be who was not a Catholic. I could see my new religion as a problem for his mother to accept. I became disillusioned with my new church when my mother took up with a priest who made sexual advances towards me. Now I began questioning all my beliefs and exploring further outside the expectations of the culture I was raised in. I wanted to go beyond religious dogma and know if God and more than the physical world existed. I developed a deep curiosity that I followed to new beliefs.

After we married, my husband was offered a job as an Industrial Engineer at United Airlines in California. California seemed to be filled with people who had left their home states and families to explore new ideas and lifestyles. I was emboldened to take the initiative to connect with people I did not know. My son was born, and I began my journey of activism.

The Creative Initiative
Foundation (CIF)

Jay Thorwaldson wrote on
Palo Alto Online, February
26, 2011, "For 60 years, the
organization went through a
dynamic process of shifting
its focus and creating spin-
off efforts that focused on
what some involved saw as
an attempt at unification
of science and religion,
following in the philosophical
footprints of Pierre Teilhard
de Chardin, the Jesuit
priest-theologian and a
geologist-paleontologist of a
century ago."

Threshold Points

Three children later and
a growing discontent in our
marriage, my husband and I
attended a discussion group
called Challenge to Change, a
series from Sequoia Seminars.
The courses were led by Creative
Initiative Foundation (CIF)
facilitators. We resonated with
how their beliefs were grounded
with actions. I left my position
as Director of Fair Housing,
and we committed our lives to a
lifestyle of spiritual and personal
development, conservation, and
social action.

Sitting in circle, women and men engaged in self-
reflection and inquiry. We used the Socratic method of
questioning and were challenged to think and validate
our replies. We were guided through processes to clear our
conditioned past. Our teachers said it was important to clear
the "vehicle" so Spirit could come through. We called this
"personal work."

For a more complete history of the Global Community
actions, go on line to *The Global Community 1950--2010,
pdf.* It was the most intensive personal work available at the
time, done in circle. We each underwent leadership training,
bringing our newfound understanding of the individual and

what was needed to better the world. Moving from Spirit we then created actions to educate the public and promote social change. Among other things, the organization was credited with ending the construction of nuclear power plants.

Our close Community included both men's and women's work. I was very engaged in Women to Women Building the Earth for the Children's Sake (Build the Earth). We also created curricula and events to awaken and empower women, along with high rituals and ceremonies for which members had to prepare. The play, *Thirteen is a Mystical Number,* was a study of Eve, Mary, and Dawn, which really deepened feminine qualities and values into my spiritual enfoldment. Eve was the unconscious feminine, Mary was the sacred mother and Dawn was the new level of consciousness embracing both our strength and our softness. The new woman was to be an active participant in creating consciousness and bringing peace in the world. We were seeped in the power of personal commitment, integrity and responsibility.

I was learning from activists and was given leadership roles in planning and arranging our public events. For four years I trained and coordinated publicity for a play that acted out the evolution of humanity. I played the same roles for CIF's pageant, *Bless Man: One Earth, One Humanity, One Spirit* at the Masonic Auditorium in San Francisco. Over a thousand women, men and youth performed for over 15,000 people over five years. My job was to get us on TV, radio shows and in newspaper stories in addition to contacting key people in San Francisco and the various international embassies in the City. I often appeared myself to represent the work we were doing.

CIF History

Gelber and Cook describe The Creative Initiative Foundation in Saving the Earth. "The Creative Initiative Foundation of the 1970s was a diverse community of people dedicated to bringing about the cooperation of the races, the religions, and the nations for the well-being of all humankind. While the beginnings were primarily in Silicon Valley and the San Francisco Bay Area, families and individual participants were also working across the U.S. and in Canada."

According to the Foundation for Global Community's online history page, "Whether they were men, women, or children, the people who lived their lives in Creative Initiative participated in a totally integrated religious experience. For them, religion was not a Sunday thing, not an afterthought, not even a separate philosophical entity. Religion was the warp and woof of their existence. It informed all their thoughts and all their actions. It defined their gender identity, their marital relations, and the interaction between parents and children. The family was the first level of collective expression of their religious ideals. The community was the second."

I remember our very elaborate demonstrations promoting peace and nuclear disarmament on May 21, 1965 to the California Energy Commission. Four hundred women dressed in rainbow color polyester pantsuits led 4000+ costumed demonstrators marching single file around the State Capitol in Sacramento. After many hours of performances, speeches, and songs, the group presented petitions calling for the protection of mother earth. We used the power of ritual to bring awareness to our place in the web of life.

In 1975 I was one of 30 women from Build the Earth sent to the first United Nations' Women Conference in Mexico City. A very different time, it was an amazing view of women around the world! Women came from everywhere it seemed. It was an eye opening experience. My job, again, was to promote our participation in this extraordinary event, the first of only four of these U.N. Conferences.

This was my life for nine years. One day one of the CIF founders, Emilia Rathbun, called a meeting and announced that our Community was straying from the original concept of embodying the life and mind of Christ, and everything-- the seminars, the schools, the protests, all of it--was shutting down for a few months to see what people would do on their own and who would return. Many of us began to see what else was happening in the world. Emotional Sensitivity Training (EST) provided another look at consciousness and personal growth. A surprising number of our community left the work.

I discovered the Sage Experience. Where CIF had reconditioned me, Sage blasted me open to new understandings and concepts, confronting my belief systems and judgment. The experiences at Sage opened my mind, an exploration out of the box of tradition. Sage was a powerful, breakthrough, personal growth workshop in the early 80's. Processes that come the closest today for clearing old conditional thinking are: Avatar Training, Landmark Forum, which is an outgrowth of EST and other programs that offer extensive and deep inner work.

My husband went back to school. I went to Mt. Shasta and expanded my spiritual understanding with a teacher named Pearl Doris, of the old I AM movement. Time away from my husband and the opening I experienced in Sage gave me perspective on the lack of joy in my marriage.

Soon after we left the Community, I realized it was the group process that kept our marriage together. Leaving the Community also allowed deeper stirrings in me to be with a feminine partner. Within a short time, I met the love of my life, Georgia. Georgia lived in a small spiritually based community, far from the Hollywood Hills of her youth. I do believe I was meant to be saturated in the energies of the deep feminine, which has been buried for so long in our culture.

A New Identity

Divorce after 25 years was a transition from my old self to my new self. I was no longer dependent on a man to support me. I needed a job. I had met the owner of a recruiting firm around a fire in Mt. Shasta, and approached him months later realizing I needed to support myself. I used all my communication and networking skills and entered the corporate world as a high tech recruiter.

Over the next few years, I amazed myself by my success. Using my intuition more than my knowledge of engineering, I worked more personally with my clients. I also gained leadership roles in the company, progressing from assistant manager to manager to owner.

I worked with high-level engineers making sure they

were a good fit both technically and personality-wise for the companies with which I worked. At one level I sold people to companies, but I always felt what we did was a service for both the companies and the individuals we placed. I believe my personal coaching helped my clients, and their success helped me be financially successful for 25 years in Silicon Valley and 12 years working from my home in the foothills.

In 1988 my partner, Georgia, and I moved to the country in the foothills of the Sierra Nevada Mountains. We found a home on 4 acres of lake front property with a 26' diameter yurt. We had the perfect setting for creating a sacred space to share our desire for personal and spiritual growth. We hosted workshops, silent retreats, and held a monthly women's circle.

I began to build my network in the new community. I was always meeting women for coffee or lunch, finding out what they were doing and their interests. Now you can use social media and Meet-ups to find people with common interests. I believe, however, that personal connection is an energy exchange more difficult to achieve through email and Skype. My work in Build the Earth and my love of women's wisdom, circle ways, and connecting people and issues birthed a quarterly newsletter, *Seeing the World through Women's Eyes*, that I published for 18 years. The theme always was the same: Inspiration, motivation, education and activation.

I met Carol Hansen Grey, the Executive Director of Women of Vision and Action (WOVA) and creator of Feminine Face of Leadership Conference in 2001. Out of one of the conferences and workshops she held, the phrase Gather the Women was born. And soon Carol started receiving phone calls from women wanting to explore what we could do under that calling. Carol arranged for a weekend where we gathered women who shared "a deep passion for awakening the power of women in service of a better world." I felt compelled to attend even though I would not know anyone else in attendance.

Social media had not yet been invented, but email and web sites were available. Carol had felt motivated to register the domain name gatherthewomen, and it was the anchor for the vision. She set up an e-list for the 15 women who had come together. This was the start of the Gather the Women Global Matrix. Our initial goals included:

- Create a website which would serve as an interactive communication hub for the women of the world, where women could share news of their successes and learn from one another.
- Invite women of the world to create gatherings to commemorate March 8th, International Women's Day.
- Encourage women to create events large and small suited to their economic needs, spiritual beliefs and cultural values, posting news of their events on the website.

Eventually, this idea developed into plans for a week of events beginning March 3, 2003. The outreach was to women using the basic tools of grassroots organizing with one new twist – the internet as global communication tool.

Carol Hansen Grey, Kathe Schaff, and I, became the active core, answering e-mails and telephone inquiries from around the world. As the GTW Events Coordinator, I described our mission. "We seek not to change minds but to connect hearts and find common ground." We followed a model that "each local gathering would be self-organizing and WOVA would provide the Gather the Women website as a hub for connection." We invited women around the world to gather and celebrate International Women's Day on March 8th, 2002.

Grey's website describes the development of GTW. "GTW was launched. Without any funding and without ever having printed a brochure, the movement had reached women on every continent. By the end of our first March event, the Steering Committee had much to celebrate. The website now hosted over 4,700 women from 67 countries as registered participants and listed more than 450 events in 23 countries." Imagine what we could have done if social media had been invented then.

Through that experience and those that followed over the years, I made very sweet personal relationships with women in Uganda, Nigeria, Costa Rica, New Zealand and across the U.S. I have stayed connected to many of these women, and have acted as a mentor for women who wanted to create local GTW events and women's circles.

Women were ready to attend the First Gather the Women International Congress in San Francisco in October 2003. The Congress took Gather the Women to the next level by creating a model to involve and connect the many diverse global women's organizations. Gather the Women invited other organizations to partner in the creation of the Congress and to bring delegations of women from their networks.

The 2003 Congress was a huge success, drawing 330

women from 26 countries representing more than 25 partner organizations. Numerous ongoing collaborative projects grew from the three-day event. Women around the world still continue to gather in the Fall at the annual Congress. As of May 2016, 93 regional coordinators, established in 44 countries, are registered on the website.

In 2002, I invited women in my community to create Gather the Women of Nevada County in order to experiment with what Gather the Women could be. GTW locally has created an International Women's Day event every year to inspire, connect and motivate one another, and has held the space for women to create and attend circles. However, from my many years sitting in circle with women, doing presentations, and creating dialogues, I felt that many women did not believe they could make a difference in the world and felt powerless in bringing their voice or influences on today's issues. For many years we worked with women to empower them. One day I realized that we are empowered. The larger question before us now is how do we motivate, cooperate and mobilize that power?

I continue to believe that we must first allow a reconditioning process to work in us. If we do not, we will continue to project our fears and past wounds, directing our anger and blame on to those we see as opposition. We will be vulnerable for getting triggered easily and do and say things we might regret.

I would propose a radical politics based on the energy of love, not fear or hate. Imagine holding those who do not agree with you with love and compassion. Not an easy task but the only one that will make a difference in the long run. When we match the energy of fear and hate with the same energy, we only feed the fear and hate. When you have found a spiritual source for the actions you want to take, with discipline you can send a different vibration to the other.

We have a lot to lose, and it appears this is really women's work--to clean house. University Research professor and author Brene Brown's Facebook post on July 8, 2016 described the threats to sacred activism that women face.

> Instead of feeling hurt, we act out our hurt. Rather than acknowledging our pain, we inflict it on others. Neither hate nor blame will lead to the justice and peace that we all want - it will only move us further apart. But we can't forget that hate and blame are seductive. Anger is easier than grief. Blame is easier than real accountability. When we choose instant relief in the form of rage, we're in many ways choosing permanent grief for the world.

I encourage the reader to personalize this book. It is the only way to make it come alive in your life.

WHAT IS SACRED ACTIVISM?

> A spirituality that is only private and self-absorbed, one devoid of an authentic political and social consciousness, does little to halt the suicidal juggernaut of

history. On the other hand, an activism that is not purified by profound spiritual and psychological self-awareness and rooted in divine truth, wisdom, and compassion will only perpetuate the problem it is trying to solve, however righteous its intentions. When, however, the deepest and most grounded spiritual vision is married to a practical and pragmatic drive to transform all existing political, economic, and social institutions, a holy force – the power of wisdom and love in action – is born. This force I define as Sacred Activism.

Andrew Harvey

Three of the most powerful creators of the American culture, most influential in our lives, are politics, religion and the media. The interactions among these three powerful creators have led to a political climate that is quite different from a radical politics based on the energy of love, not fear or hate. Politics and religion are beginning to morph, and the media promotes outcomes that are the most divisive, entertaining and outside the norm as possible. In the 2016 election cycle, Donald Trump, who of course was subsequently elected President of the United States, was covered every time he sneezed at no cost to him! As a businessman and showman, he ran over the politicos. He tended to spew divisiveness. At times, his opponents matched his energy of fear and hate, and both of these toxic emotions escalated. At other times, his opponents remained quiet, and his voice was the only one heard. Even after he was elected, members of Congress from his own party remained quiet as his decisions continued to be driven by toxic emotions. I have seen no evidence of a spiritual source leading to personal development and activism propelled by the energy of love in the campaign, election, and early days of the Trump presidency.

It is tempting to see these interactions as the manifestations of men and conclude that they have all been testosterone and adrenalin driven. Certainly, the current system has been developed by men, who hold the majority of the power in our culture. We can conclude that values of competition, immediacy, winning and short-term goals are strictly gender based. But not all men by any means adhere to these values. Rather than assigning them a gender identity, it seems more accurate to attribute these values to a particular type of power structure: Patriarchy. Yes, identical values can apply to women who have assumed these traits to succeed in the patriarchal structure. Indeed, women intent on playing the patriarchal game can tend to work even harder at assuming these traits having been conditioned to believe they must use the patriarchal structure to achieve their success.

As I will fully explain in subsequent sections of this book, women are making strides since gaining the vote in 1920. But patriarchy continues to be deeply embedded in the psyche of our humanity. The missing ingredient in the world is that more than half of the population has been dismissed from power and influence. Even today the most powerful women we know deal with the internal voice of the father, affecting their confidence and creating sexual confusion when men continue to objectify them. The internal voice from the mother passes on the many restrictions placed on women from generation to generation.

I understand younger women under 40 tend to avoid thinking in terms of gender, a lovely idea. I would, however, question if we are able to do that yet. While it is a goal to have partnership on equal terms, I have not witnessed that occurring generally speaking. As long as sexual harassment, the subtleties of misogyny, rape on campus and in the military still find young men acting out the age old messages of entitlement in patriarchy, we have work to do.

Feminism is not a bad word, but one that must be redeemed using today's issues. The women who started this movement angry were outraged over centuries of female repression. I can now celebrate the changes that have come from the hard work and sacrifices of women before us. However, issues remain. There is a wonderful power in feminism, in its history and in the beautiful men who have also identified with the word.

As women, we can look over our own stories as I have and see the direct influence and impact patriarchy has had on our lives. I have lived as the classic suburban housewife of the 50's who could not get a bank loan in her own name or credit without my husband's signature. Younger women have reaped the benefit of those who have come before. Without knowledge of history, important issues can become more subtle and acceptable without recognition of the work that is yet to be completed.

I do believe sisterhood is important in order for us to gain critical mass. It can support us in moving from the old paradigm of women in competition with one another, lacking trust and based on old male models, to joining in sisterhood with one another. When women come together, we are more global, inclusive, cooperative and relational. Garzena and D'Antonia, authors of *The Athena Doctrine*, share statistics showing that women's businesses are increasingly more successful based on these principles. Indeed, all businesses are beginning to see the worth of women's values and ways of doing business. Global values lead us to ask, "What impact does this decision have in the long run? How will it affect the larger community?" Valuing inclusiveness, we seek for approaches that use the unique talents of individuals. Behaving cooperatively, we value compromise. Relational values prompt us to ask, "How can we connect to each other and our environment?"

We see the effects of sisterhood now in Congress, where the Republican and Democratic women meet for lunch to share their personal lives and perspectives with one another. Together they actually avoided a government shut down, by working with one another to reach agreement. The October 16, 2013 *Time* article by Jay Newton-Small summed it up, "Women are the only adults left in Washington."

The Energetics Of Activism

Surprisingly, I learned over the years that activism creates fields of energy. What do I mean? When I began my activism in my 20's, I was usually frustrated and angry. And I hung out with those people who shared my complaints and upsets. Then I began to understand the power of our thoughts and the use of our energy. I recognized that the win or lose game really doesn't bring about much change.

The postures that we take in politics and religion

communicate that we are right and they are wrong. They must agree with us or be eliminated! We tend to find those who agree with us, and together we make "the other" wrong and to isolate ourselves from them. The ones who agree with us are the people with whom we are in relationship. Indeed, some become like family. But when we cling to those who agree with us and isolate ourselves from those who do not, we tend to recycle the same thoughts and ideas.

Imagine if we could take a stand in the world and yet have no enemies? Imagine holding those who disagree with us in love and compassion, praying for their well-being. What if we really embodied concepts like forgiveness and love of others? What would that look like? It might look like meeting the basic needs of everyone, and honoring the differences we have. Many years ago, our members of Congress actually got together after a day of arguing, bickering if you will, and went out for a drink or a card game afterwards. Friendships developed that crossed the aisle. Now, we find ourselves in a world where we are alienated from one another and lacking in consideration, respect and openness. And yet we still speak of love and forgiveness.

This book comes from the perspective that change in the world does begin with you and me. The power of our thoughts and words do create our world. In 1903, James Allen wrote in "As a Man Thinketh" (the use of the word "man" reflects the era), "[We] think in secret, and it comes to pass. Environment is but [our] looking glass." Today's cutting edge quantum physics and mastery wisdom traditions agree.

"In the beginning was the Word…" John 1:1 King James Version (KJV)

"And the Word was made flesh…" John 1:14 King James Version (KJV)

Every thought, word, and deed is a prayer. What are these statements implying? We have power to create. Look around your room. Every human made thing began first as a thought and then was made manifest.

So how much of the violence, the terror and the fear are our creation? How did we create ISIS? Bad politicians? Perhaps we might consider the thoughts we have held, projected out, spoken to as a creative force, based on the fears we buy into and act on. In fact we are a part of a collective of creative forces. Even if you did not participate personally, you are in a field of energy that we have all contributed to. It is from this field of energy that our reality is created.

In this political environment we can see reflected back to us what we have created out of anger, fear, judgment, hate and separation. We tend to separate ourselves from these negative feelings, believing that we are good and gentle beings, and that the negativity and upsets are not of our doing. We feed one another. "Aren't they terrible?" "Don't trust any of them." And then we wonder why there is so much mistrust and conflict in the world around us! "Who me? I'm not responsible."

There is a big difference between judgment and discernment. Discernment should be about making our own personal choices. What will forward our visions and support our values? On the other hand, our judgments create separation. We lose the opportunity to expand our compassion and acceptance. These reflections apply to all humans, so why am I calling on women to wake the world?

What Is Sacred Activism for Women?

Activists are people who see the need for change, improvement, and motivation on a large scale. They are people driven by passion, keen to share facts they want understood more widely, and led by a vision for a better future. Activism comes naturally to some, while for others, it's something that is thrust upon them as a result of particular experiences or upon learning about something they passionately believe needs to change. Whatever your reason for wanting to become an activist, you have the ability to do so no matter your age, your means, your time or your background. Having the belief that you can make a difference helps give you the power to do something at the heart of creating change for the better.

Why Women? A woman engaged in sacred activism is sourced from feminine values, walks her talk, and does not blame or demonize those who do not share her convictions. She comes from an inner connection with Source. Sacred activism requires conviction, confidence and courage. Conviction is the stand she is taking. Confidence allows her to act on the stand she is taking. Courage allows her to be vulnerable and to be willing to speak her truth.

Women need to be at the table, from the kitchen table to the table of global consequences. Sister Joan Chittister, Benedictine nun, author and lecturer, was asked in an interview with Oprah, "What do you want to see changed in the world?" She replied, "Nothing will change in the world until the situation of women changes." Chittister continues,

You cannot simply dismiss half of the human race, which means dismiss their agendas, dismiss their needs, dismiss their gifts, dismiss their intelligence. We are now at the place where men are running everything, which means that humanity is seeing with one eye, hearing with one ear, and thinking with one half of the human brain . . . .We are bringing to the table only half the needs of the human race!

I don't mean that men are doing this purposively; it's just that they only have half of the human experience. They have half the wisdom. They have half the intelligence. So they are making full decisions out of half of the resources that we should have . . . .Who gets left behind? The poorest of the poor-- women and children.

This is why women must step up if we are to have a future for our children and grandchildren. These are not the typical conversations men have, particularly older men. Men talk about how things work, and what they can do, rather than what they can be. It is more comfortable for them to address things not people. We must remind them to care for people before things; to share power with others, not hold power over them.

Why NOT women? The decision makers who have created our systems and institutions and plundered the earth for 5000 years have been men. Women's voices and influence have been historically ignored and eliminated. We are now seeing the unsustainability of our current systems and culture and the need to include the wisdom of the female brain and relational thinking. Now is the time for women to reclaim, honor, and bring the feminine perspective to professions, businesses, religious organizations, and public sectors.

Issues Women Face

When we talk about women's issues, men leave the room! Not their problem; they're women's issues. If we are talking about hysterectomies, divorce, or single motherhood - these are women's issues.

However, if we are referring to unequal pay, rape, domestic abuse, sex trafficking, or lack of women in office or higher management positions or on Boards of influence - these are men's issues. It is important to avoid the term "women's issues." First of all, it lets men off the hook because it doesn't sound like their issues, therefore becoming unimportant. Women may have to navigate and work their way through these issues, but they are created by the actions and obstacles that men initiated. Here we are talking about women's rights and men's responsibilities.

Women, All Sisters, Remember?   -Jane Evershed

Act like you already
Manage a nation.
Summon your purpose
With your heart's conviction
And take your station.

You are being nudged
By earth-necessity
To resurrect humanity
And mold it
With your hands
Gentle and strong
Into a sculpture of sanity.
Come on.

You can no longer carry
The rage, fury and weep,
Of fire, storm and flood,
The seeping of shed blood.
You have been
Missing In Action
Lured way off track,

By instigated distraction.
Hurl your "lesser than"
All the way back
To Minoan Crete
Risk your life,
Gather a clan,
Take the reigns,
Take to the street.

There is global warming
And war to defeat.
And a host of heinous crimes
Which render woman as meat,
To tenderize, to use, to enter,
To traffic, stone and burn.
When will we learn?
Woman, all sisters
Remember your power
It is for earth healing
That we yearn.
This is the eleventh hour
Scour, Scurry, Scour.

Leap of Faith by Jane Evershed

What kind of action for change can you initiate or support?

Self-Reflection #1: What Does Sacred Activism Mean to Me?

Sacred Activism is the fusion of sacred consciousness, passion, generosity and peace with wise radical action. Finding ways to serve humanity and the Earth through Sacred Activism opens the way for birthing the new paradigm of heart centered consciousness in the world. - Andrew Harvey

Do I resonate with this quote?

How do I integrate my consciousness and passion in the actions I am taking?

SACRED ACTIVISM: YOUR TURN!

I've told my story and examined the general characteristics of Sacred Activism. I've shared why I believe it is a particularly powerful approach to life for women. But, how can you embody the thoughts and actions here? I have prepared a graphic to help to lead you through this section and the choices you make to become a sacred activist. The headings in the graphic match the headings in this next section. We encourage you to refer back again and again to the diagram as you read the following suggestions.

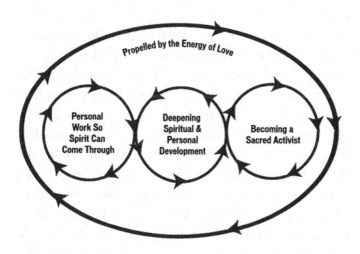

Graphic by Barbara Bitner

Personal Work So Spirit Can Come Through

You may recall that I was unable to acquire a college education because of my injuries in a serious train wreck. Without formal education and theories, I instead developed my inner senses and a desire to communicate. I now appreciate how my life situations allowed me time for deep thinking and questioning. If you are engaging in the issues women specifically have to deal with, there are many personal areas to examine.

How are your relationships with the men in your life? If you are hurt or angry, you will appear to be male-bashing or seeking a matriarchy to replace patriarchy. Unhealed tones of voice or victim-mentality may shut down your listeners. Speaking from wholeness will encourage others to embrace your goal or message. Partnership begins with two whole human beings who offer respect, and value the gifts and skills of the other.

Look deeply and be honest about the inequality between men and women in our society. Become aware of and speak to what you see around you. Patriarchal beliefs can be very subtle and appear totally acceptable to everyone around you. Look with new eyes at what dominant male rule has embedded in both genders. Bring awareness to conversations and actions that devalue female bodies, needs, skills, and dreams; or devalue male emotions, vulnerability or support of feminine values. Most women have an inner father's voice that says, "That's not ladylike. Men are in charge. Leave it to the men." The inner mother's voice says, "Be a good girl. Be nice. Let John win. Let Mike speak first. Say the right thing and support the men." We have to identify the voices in our heads and say, "Thank you for sharing, but I will do what is authentic for me."

Watch your language. We assume everyone has the

same meaning for the words they use. Not necessarily so. Check it out "When you say….,what do you mean when you use that word or sentence?" Clarify. It is important to realize that men finalized language from the experiences of men. Dictionaries were compiled by studying how words were used in published writings, which were written primarily by men. See *The Meaning of Everything* for the fascinating story of the development of the *Oxford English Dictionary* and Dale Spender's *Man Made Language.* The language available to us is from their experiences, not ours. Perhaps that is why it takes longer for women to express what they mean. At times, we throw up our hands and admit, "I don't have the words."

Compare how women and Earth are treated. Has our connection with the Feminine been purposely broken? Look at your relationship to the ultimate Mother, Earth. Notice the relationship between the devaluation of the Feminine and the degradation of the Earth, the abuse of women, their exclusion from influence, and ultimately the decline of all life.

Deepening Personal and Spiritual Development

The deepening of my personal and spiritual development began when I joined CIF. I've described sitting in circle with men and women to engage in self-reflection and inquiry. Using the Socratic method of questioning, we were challenged to think and validate our replies. It was the most intensive personal work done at this time. My story, however, describes this deepening as ongoing and indeed continues to this day. How would you like to deepen your personal and spiritual development?

Tap into your full strength. Embrace all parts of yourself to access strength. Reflection, meditation, openness to change and prayer are portals to your inner strength. Call on your inner strength to deliver your message, your ideas and solutions. Speak with confidence and conviction without apologies. Love and self- acceptance are critical to making a difference in the world.

Confidence is a quality that many of us lack. I remember when a man speaking on the radio was talking about our differences as men and women. He said, "When a man speaks he does so with confidence, even if he is wrong. Women often speak without confidence, even when they are right." Ever notice how often women say, "I'm sorry, excuse me," or "May I say something here?" Does this resonate with you? You might want to read the *Confidence Code* by Katty Kay and Claire Shipman. It takes **courage** to break the patterns of silence, of staying safe. A great way to gain courage is to practice! Say what you are thinking even if it differs from the norm. Find a women's circle to sit with other women finding their own courage. Speak from and listen with **compassion**. Practice by deep listening to people who share the same beliefs and feel as strongly as you do. Then listen with the same compassion to those who do not agree with you. Ask questions not to change them but to understand how they came to their opinion.

Build coalitions/connect. Seek out other women or organizations that hold similar positions on the issues you care about. Or perhaps support common ground whenever possible with those who hold different positions. For example, anti abortion and pro choice have a major disagreement in how to approach unwanted pregnancies. They do, however, agree there is a need to support young people in avoiding pregnancy. Together they can make an impact. There is always strength in numbers. Coalition building comes with challenges and opportunities to work them out and for your own personal growth. Focus on commonalities, not differences.

To be creative, we must think out of the box. Look for new approaches, new ways of seeing things. A great resource is a book called *Do You Quantum Think?* by Diane Collins. She provides effective tools for shifting perspectives.

How are you communicating your message? How do you rate yourself as a speaker or presenter? How frustrating is it to feel passionate about an issue and not be able to express it clearly? Is your voice and message being received? It could be helpful to join a Toastmasters Club or other speaker's training. You can learn to speak authentically and inspire action with your message. Increase your ability to take positive action and to educate, inspire and invite women to participate with you. Do your own research to support the truth.

Don't be afraid of leadership. So often women pull back when called on for leadership. It is important to remember that this word has been modeled primarily by men who express leadership as power over others. Women already are natural leaders in their homes and families, communities, churches, and schools or work places. It is time for us to step outside our comfort zones into public leadership. I woke up one morning and realized, we really must mother the world now. We must want for the world what we want for our children. Good health, good education, good clean environments, and respect for others. We must start living our values (not preaching them) as inspired and loving human beings.

A leader using the feminine model stands in her truth and power and moves from authenticity. She is not afraid to admit when she is wrong and has no need to defend her ego; therefore she generates harmony instead of fear. She is one who is inclusive and empowers those around her. Consequently she finds herself in the company of other leaders. She is both the teacher and the student. She is confident, courageous, collaborative, creative, and is a good communicator open to expand, to take in new information and to listen deeply.

Another word to examine would be "follower." A follower is one who has given her power to another or others. There is always a price to pay for doing so, one of which is to lose a sense of self, of confidence. We can get quite good at repeating words we've heard, but our voice becomes authentic when we speak from our own truth.

Self Reflection #2: Going Deeper

Consider the following: How might you begin with a personal processing of old beliefs, old conditioning? A journal is a good start where you can begin to examine your motivations, intentions, and outcomes.

Where and who in your life needs to be forgiven? For lack of forgiveness does no real harm to the other, but it will drain you of energy.

What belief "systems" do you live by without questioning them? Question them!

How good are your listening skills?

Do you react or respond?

Do you remember to ask questions of the other?

Becoming a Sacred Activist

For me, this step began with the actions I took long ago in Palo Alto to change how people interacted and to build understanding and respect between people. I reached out to people with a shared desire for change and peace, working with the YWCA to create home visit exchanges. Black and white families went to each other's homes to see the human sameness of our families. Repeatedly, I have been involved in Sacred Activism. You can read about my most recent work with Indivisible in a section to follow. Having engaged in personal work so that spirit could shine through and deepening your personal and spiritual development, what spiritually driven actions could you take?

Initially you must take a personal inventory. Take time to explore where you are in your life. How much time, energy and resources do you intend for activism? What is manageable?

We are all at different stages of our lives. Are you dependent on your parents and/or other support? Are you engaged in a full-time job as well as being a part time activist or does your activism support you? If you have a family, your children's ages are important to take into consideration. Is good parenting your sacred activism? Are you an elder with time and financial resources to support your own or another's activism?

I mentioned in my story Creative Initiative kept me in touch with my priorities. Make a list of everything currently in your daily routines and on your calendar. Include your personal and spiritual/religious practices including time with family and friends, and activities for health, wellness, and recreation. Include work/activism/income-producing activities and volunteer time for groups and meetings. Next prioritize. Group 1: Does the activity support you and your passion? Yes! Necessary for supporting my wellbeing. Group 2: Does it drain you? Is it a habit or should? Consider if you could replace any activities in group 2 with time for activism.

Consider if you have the time and resources to invest in your own campaign or if working with an established group or inviting others to join you would achieve your goals more efficiently. Find out who is already doing things for your cause at the local, regional, national or international level. Why reinvent the wheel? Where can you plug in? Perhaps you can duplicate successful efforts from another location or join a group that needs more hands. If you are starting your own group, get organized!

Fuel your passion. When I saw something that I felt needed fixing, the desire to change it took hold of me. It's like when you have a thought of buying a new car, you see that model everywhere. Thought or awareness leads to desire, passion, and responsibilities. Do your personal clearing and spiritual practices to continue connecting to your true passion. Take responsibility for your thoughts and patterns. Be alert of traps, detours, and negativity from inside and outside. Negativity will eat you up and change nothing. Continue to visualize the outcome you want to achieve or contribute to. Inspire others to do the same. Acknowledge and celebrate every step and success. One person - you - can make a difference.

Self-care is critical. Support your activism with a healthy body. Practice nonviolence with yourself. For example, self-criticism is not helpful, but evaluating one's behaviors in ways that support compassionate and positive change should be a non-violent process. In your personal/spiritual work, stay aware of your physical needs and emotions. Notice your levels of patience, tolerance and kindness. If you crash and burn or become angry and reactive, you will not be able to relate in the moment to your family, peers, or opponents. You will be letting yourself down and all those that depend on you.

While you may want to think big, small gradual steps may be more sustainable. Change is necessary at every level. Choose a step that leads in that direction. What steps can you add to your calendar today? In 30 days? In one year? Be kind to yourself as you walk your path.

Can you allow for the steps you must take and let go of attachment of achieving the end goal? As all the activist before you would remind you, you may never see the end results. Amanda Sussman, a successful advocate for policy change, asks, "Are you happy with striving for an ideal, even if you never reach it? Do you need to see immediate progress, even if it's small, to keep you going?" Understanding what your needs are and how to take care of yourself will guide you to the actions that are yours to do.

Know your gifts, skills and preferences for working with others. Do you know your strengths? Read about strengths or take a strength survey online. Optimize what you do best. Consider writing, teaching, speaking, planning events, creating art. Do you have online skills of website building, blogging or leading podcasts?

Do you prefer people or projects? How are your people and conflict resolution skills? If you prefer people and you are working alone and not able to sustain your passion, find a group that works for your issue. There are many opportunities for individual activism using online social networking.

What do you stand for? Do you have an affirmative vision, one that shows what you stand for, not just what you're against? What are your concerns and what solutions do you want to work towards? Create your message based on your vision.

As a sacred activist, do you have a clear and consistent message? Does your core group share your vision, values and concerns? Are you willing to work together and resolve conflicts while staying focused on the vision for the highest good? What will you feed energetically both within and outside your group?

Learn to deal with conflict. People will react in ways that are not always considerate or constructive when you challenge the status quo, Even groups with a shared vision see different paths of action. There are many forms of negativity. This is an opportunity to provide healthier examples. Work on your people skills and learn conflict resolution or non-violent communication. Read "Embracing Conflict" in Gloria Feldt's *No Excuses*.

Become an expert on your issue or concern. Read widely within the cause itself, to understand the issues clearly and to learn about the tactics, ideas, experiences, wins and losses, and other useful information from those who have already been active in the cause. Be sure to include women activists and learn how they chose to overcome obstacles. Then, read books or befriend those that have the opposite view from yours. Relate human to human. What makes them tick? Why do they believe what they do? Practice listening and asking questions. Explore livingroomconversations. org. Initiate conversations around your concerns and dive deeper into other's experiences with the subject. Come from curiosity rather than debating or arguing your point.

Learn how to use and work with the media. Activism derives power from its ability to educate, raise awareness, and make people passionate about an issue. Research the facts and legislation for your cause to build credibility. Team up with folks who know how to write press releases and editorials and contact the press. Become knowledgeable of the local laws and permits necessary for public actions.

Create a plan and get your message out. Write a strategic plan and action steps. Schedule meetings or actions. Reserve locations, get permits, and know the laws. Record your message from your heart, create YouTubes and post them. Be ready to spread the word through social media: Twitter, Facebook, meetup.com, forums, email lists, zoom video conference calls and newsletters. Introduce yourself and your message to groups you belong to with fliers, table-sits, and phone trees. Face-to-face contact, even if online, is the best way to build connections with people interested in your cause. Let people know they are needed/wanted in a group. If your group is large, create subcommittees, for example: public relations, outreach, logistics, and finances.

If you don't have social media skills, team up with those that do.

Don't forget change begins within you first. This important point bears repeating. If you have anger or if you are depressed or if you feel you have to go to war against something - STOP. Do your own inner work first. These feelings will only work against your vision. Meeting war with war, anger with anger only creates more war and anger. It can stop with you. Your message won't be heard. Transform any negativity including frustration and anger into fuel for creative responses. Don't make the other – other. Become a peace maker. Instead, ask yourself, "How am I like that? Do I have that trait within me?" Take responsibility for your thoughts, patterns, and reactions. Acknowledge and celebrate yourself when you do.

Speak out and speak up with confidence and courage. Be willing to be embarrassed! When you step out of the expected or the norm in any area you will stir people. When you do that you know you are doing something right!

Consider positions of leadership in your community to increase your sphere of influence. Check your city, county, and state offices/websites for openings and appointments to commissions and boards. If you have some experience under your belt in public service, consider higher office. We end with this very important goal: to bring women into positions of leadership and influence.

Heart of a Visionary by Shiloh Sophia McCloud

Visionary Work

The work of a visionary is to know the past, dream the future and take action in the present.

We create a path where there are no paths, lay groundwork where no ground lays.
We see behind the veil of impossible/possible and we do not let our fear stop us.

We do not follow the agenda
or the status quo or those "in the know". No.

Our way is uncharted territory
at the gateway where the worlds meet.
The work of a visionary is
to know the past, dream the future
and take powerful action in the present.

~ Shiloh Sophia McCloud

SACRED ACTION

To reiterate, the first step for sacred action is being aware of where you are sourcing the stand you are taking--from love or from fear? We have suggested you will get further if you can come from respect for the other, holding for them their highest good and yours. Even when you do not like or approve of their behavior or opinion, you wish them no harm. Even if they don't change, you continue to love them. Rather than resisting what you don't want, consider spending your time and energy on what you do want.

There are really two forms of action. The one we are focusing on here is speaking to power. Avoid using the dominant patriarchal model (power over others). Center in and explore your feminine insights, your heart and body's messages, and relational reasoning.

However, your neighbor or your friends who oppose your views may not be changed by your newly found articulation. Be willing to have the conversations we are supposed to avoid. This perhaps is the most difficult of actions. Listen and ask questions. Get personal. Hear their stories. You might share your own. Ask them their concerns about your position. And then ask if they would like to hear your concerns about their position. They can hear respect. They can hear caring. Facts seldom work, as you each have your own belief systems and facts. Relationship works. Be bold and vulnerable.

Specific Actions You Can Take

In larger arenas where you are not able to form personal relationships easily, we encourage women to find other ways to speak out and to speak up. Here are some specific actions that can make a difference. It does not have to be a slow process for women to bring their skills to the table of global consequences. It is long overdue.

- Sign a Petition. Are they useful or not? You can find opinions on both sides. Signing is one quick and easy to do action. You are telling the "universe" you care!!!
- Start a petition. Change.org, https://petitions.whitehouse.gov, http://www.thepetitionsite.com/create-a-petition.html
- Support an organization or campaign financially. Your contributions do count. Groups rely on monthly contributions to survive. Even your $5 or $10 can make a difference to pay the phone bill.
- Call or write old-fashioned letters to Congress people with your point of view. No blame, no shame, just a vision of the possible. Phone calls and mailed letters still hold more weight than emails in politics.
- Volunteer for openings in your community/county boards. Bring your feminine voice, ideas and values to provide balance to male dominated boards.
- Step forward as a candidate for elected office or find someone to support with time and or money.

- Join a group that reflects your values and perspectives. You may be the one who offers a different perspective. Notice the difference between "taking a stand for or holding your vision" and "taking down the enemy." Replace the language and tactics of war, e.g., fight, demolish, win, etc. with creating a new way, with being solution oriented. Initiate the unpopular, "don't go there" kind of conversation if you can do so without anger, without name-calling.

- Listen! Ask questions about their belief and thought process. Where do they get their facts and information? What frightens them about what you believe? What was the experience that brought them to that conclusion?

- Be an online activist. Post responses to others opinions…. diplomatically. Post your own opinions. Use Facebook, Twitter and other social media outlets. Create a blog and respond to other blogs. Your ideas matter. This is both an important way to participate and perhaps even the easiest. Take a stand and educate your friends and followers.

- From ISIL to the other political party, send "them" love! If you pray, pray for them. If you can send positive thoughts do so. Not to change their minds, but to open both your heart and their hearts. Remember every thought, every word and every action is a prayer. What are you praying for?

- Be informed! Do your homework. Seek to inspire.

A Principle for Sacred Activism

Never complain or speak about an issue without offering a solution or taking an action towards its resolution.

Marilyn Rosenbrock Nyborg

Self-Care to Balance Negativity

How do we sustain and maintain a positive attitude in a world awash with negativity, anger and violence? Here are some ways to consider. Surround yourself with meaning, art, symbols and photos of those you love. Fill your home with music that you find inspiring, uplifting and fun. Monitor your thinking. When it feels you are overwhelmed with negativity, take a break for infill. There are endless teleconferences, poetry, podcasts, and TED talks. Use them! Balance yourself. If you give 10% of your time to activism, take 10% of your time to be inspired. Take time for yourself and your loved ones.

Marilyn Rosenbrock Nyborg

Self Reflection #3: What Can I Do?

In her interview with Sister Joan Chittister Oprah asked, "What can we do?" Sister's quick response was simple, "SOMETHING!"

What is my something? What is my passion? What is the next step for me?

What am I committed to?

What stops me? What are my "buts?"

Who do my connections know that might be interested in my projects or ideas?

Successful Actions to Duplicate

Indivisible Women. After the 2016 election I asked my friend, Barbara DeHart, what we could do for all the grieving women in our community. The women were in shock that a man so disrespectful of so many groups of people including half the population who are women was elected to the highest office in the land instead of a qualified woman. We initiated a conversation in my living room with thirty-three women. My friend Elisa Parker, founder of See Jane Do, joined Barbara and me as co-founders ready to take the lead. We based our organizing on *The Indivisible Guide,* which gives detailed instructions for organizing actions to hold our representatives accountable. Indivisible Women (IW) was born.

Barbara created an IW Facebook page and invited women to our first public event. The weather was so bad we did not think anyone would show up. We drove to the venue in pounding rain and wind with trees literally falling down, to share that the meeting was cancelled. We were truly surprised as women kept arriving. We knew if a storm did not stop 40 women, we had to do something to direct their passion to action. We listened to each other and wrote down the main concerns of the group. The next gathering would be formed into interest groups to develop plans of actions. Women invited women. 350 women showed up at the third gathering. Nearly 600 showed up at the fourth event. Our Facebook page grew to over 3000 friends in 8 months. We continue to stand as Indivisible Women holding women together in a community for the many reasons mentioned in this book.

Channeling anger, fear, and hopelessness into creative action is not impossible. We started our gatherings with quieting the mind and centering in our hearts. When women listen to each other, laugh together, and tap into their inner wisdom, they collectively release hormones of oxytocin, dopamine and serotonin that relax fear and stress, open communication and allow collaboration. We also agreed to focus on women only and allow them a safe platform to express their ideas and opinions.

Claiming a space to support women's sacred activism is not always easy. Both women and men question our choice. Men did show up to the third meeting, and some understood it was for women. One angry man demonstrated male entitlement as he demanded to be included. I was more intent on getting every woman who showed up into the standing room only space. After the meeting, a response to him came to me. "Your hostility and inability to hear the reasons I offer are why we prefer women only here." I often respond to the question, "Why don't you include men?" with "Women need their space and support to find their voices and not compete with men's need to speak." Women have their issues and men have their issues. Men are free to initiate their own group. My hope is that both grow clear and learn to stand side by side. I have concluded this book with a letter to men.

Living Room Conversations.

Indivisible Women members created twelve teams that focus on interest groups. Since my interest is in listening and finding connections, I invited women to a group, Reaching Across the Aisle. I had discovered Living Room Conversations created by Joan Blades, founder of MoveOn.

org and MomsRising, and other dialogue experts. The format was designed to

> empower everyday citizens to discuss important issues with friends of differing political affiliations and backgrounds. The theory was that if two friends with different points of view, each invited two friends to join a conversation, with full disclosure about the intent and structure of the conversation, they could create a safe space for a respectful and meaningful exchange of ideas, develop new relationships and perhaps find common ground.

> We actually avoid debate, dialog and the issues of the day, focusing instead on values and underlying beliefs. The website http://www.livingroomconversations.org provides all the details including how to facilitate this model and topic scripts.

I have found the model is less conversational than deep listening between both like-minded people as well as those with opposing viewpoints. It is also a doorway to reopening relationships we have abandoned with people who disagree with our political views. Our IW group meets together to experience the format and what shows up in ourselves so that each of us gains confidence in hosting a LRC. Some of us react quickly to trigger words or make assumptions about people and are afraid of how we are perceived. Observing our fight, flight or freeze survival patterns and how to calm our minds and bodies are important skills in interacting in our culture. Connecting to our authentic self and spiritual courage allows us to express our voice. Developing our intra and interpersonal skills will give us confidence to claim our right to be at any table.

There is an enormous desire and need for person-to-person conversations and relationships not via text or email. Similar programs are popping up across the nation. I also see a need to involve more community members quickly to counteract the growing violence in our country. LRC provides guidelines for Faith communities which can also be applied to large groups. At this time I am planning to expand the 6 person group to a larger venue with tables of 4-6 people creating listening cafes. My goal is to connect hearts, not necessarily change minds.

I invite you to visit the Living Room Conversations website and invite a few friends to join you. If you follow the ground rules, you may be surprised at what comes up in the group. Your group can continue with other topics or branch out and invite people from across the aisle. Whichever you choose, you will be examining your beliefs and practicing deeper listening without defending or debating.

The Male Champions of Change. Elizabeth Broderick created The Male Champions of Change, a measurable plan for male leadership to advocate and act to increase the number of women in leadership positions. She began with the hypothesis that gender imbalance is a social and economic issue that male leaders need to address.

"In most nations, men largely occupy the seats of power. Relying exclusively on women to lead change on gender equality is therefore illogical. We need decent, powerful men to step up beside women to create a more gender equal world." ~ Elizabeth Broderick, Sex Discrimination Commissioner of Australia

Here's what she did. She called the top 25 male leaders in Australia from CEO's of major corporations, government officials, and the military. She met with them individually and basically asked them to speak for women to the men they managed. They discussed women's power and how they responded to it. They discussed their fears and concerns about women in power. They went back and met with other men. The group also took on men's violence against women; higher expectations of men; and updating policies to address gender harassment throughout the military.

In a message responding to the issues and heralding the Army's intent to overhaul the culture, personnel, policies and practices that enabled such behavior to occur, General David Morrison, Chief of Army, publicly and firmly told his troops, "there is simply no place for that type of behavior in this army." He reminded the leaders, "that the standard you walk past is the standard you accept".

This program could be initiated in every community starting with the men who lead. The Male Champions of Change website details how to *Start a Group*. We need to ask men to be our heroes to take a stand for our safety and for our inclusion into leadership. Who could research the companies or agencies in their community for the number of women serving on their boards of directors? Letters of appreciation could be sent to those who have gender balance. Where gender balance is lacking, it could be pointed out that they are missing the value of women's input and perspective. In *The Athena Doctrine,* Gerzema and D'Antonio have shown that when women are involved in business at the senior levels, the businesses do better!

Join or Create Cities for CEDAW. In 1979 the United Nations General Assembly adopted the Convention on the Elimination of All Forms of Discrimination against Women (CEDAW). It defines what constitutes discrimination against women and sets up an agenda for national action to end such discrimination. In 1980, President Carter signed CEDAW. However it was not made law by Congress. As of January 2016, Iran, South Sudan, Somalia and the United States, as the only Western and industrialized democracy, have not ratified CEDAW.

CEDAW defines discrimination against women as "... any distinction, exclusion or restriction made on the basis of sex which has the effect or purpose of impairing or nullifying the recognition, enjoyment or exercise by women, irrespective of their marital status, on a basis of equality of men and women, of human rights and fundamental freedoms in the political, economic, social, cultural, civil or any other field."

CEDAW includes equal pay for men and women; for maternity leave with pay; for policies that enable parents to balance family obligations with work responsibilities; as well as for special workplace protections for pregnant women. The U.N. Working Group on discrimination against women in law and practice concluded, "The United States lags behind human rights standards in protecting women's rights. There are missing rights and protections, especially regarding pregnant workers and workers with caregiving responsibilities."

Currently, the U.S. is the only industrialized country that fails to ensure workers are provided paid parental leave. As a result, only 12 per cent of the private sector workforce is eligible for paid family leave, offered voluntarily by their employer. Yes, that means the majority of working women do not have access to paid family leave when they have a baby. This has real and tangible psychological, physical, emotional, and economic consequences. The U.S. also fails to provide paid leave to care for ill family members, and there is no national guarantee of paid sick time.

The refusal of the United States Congress to ratify CEDAW has led to local actions that will move the principles forward. In 1998, San Francisco became the first city in the world to adopt a CEDAW ordinance into city and county governance establishing *the Department* on the Status of Women. Los Angeles followed in 2003.

An organized plan for passing ordinances establishing the principles of CEDAW in cities and towns across the United States began at a meeting of *The UN Commission on the Status of* Women in 2013. Since then, the NGO Committee on the Status of Women in New York, the Women's Intercultural Network (WIN) and The Leadership Conference on Civil and Human Rights (in conjunction with The Leadership Conference Education Fund) have developed *Cities for CEDAW.*

The Cities for CEDAW "...campaign is a grassroots effort

that provides tools and leadership to empower local women's, civil and human rights organizations and municipalities to effectively initiate CEDAW within their city, county, town, or state."

> "Cities for CEDAW's goal for 100 cities to adopt a CEDAW measure *was* supported at the June 2014 U.S. Conference of Mayors mobilizing elected officials, the media, business, youth, NGOs, faith communities, and women leaders. The campaign focuses on the adoption of a CEDAW measure that fulfills three requirements – a gender analysis of city operations (workforce, programs, budget), an oversight body, and funding to support the implementation of the principles of CEDAW."

Become familiar with all the information and tools for introducing CEDAW and Cities for CEDAW. Look for and collaborate with the major stakeholders in your community to pass a measure. One city at a time we will move forward.

Taking Sacred Activism into Radical Politics

If you apply this Guide to your life and have a sense of where your passion lies and how you might like to participate in making a difference in your life, your community, your state and the world, you are ready for radical politics. Radical politics is particularly needed if we are going to make the necessary changes to address complex issues like climate change.

According to Wikipedia, "Politics: from Greek: πολιτικός politikos, definition 'of, for, or relating to citizens' is the practice and theory of influencing other people on a civic or individual need." Mainstream politicians tend to use war language to affect change. They identify the enemy, create a plan of attack, and attack the person as well as the ideas or beliefs. This approach to attacking that with which we do not agree has escalated in the last several decades.

Because of the possibility of initiating a political war, our culture has encouraged us to avoid any conflicting conversations with those who disagree with us politically and to hang out with like-minded people. There was a time in Washington when our elected representatives could argue loudly on the floor of the Congress and then share a meal or go golfing together. We have lost that capacity, the capacity for relationship, and it has led us down a very dangerous road.

Compromise is a lost art. As Rush Limbaugh once said on the radio, "You can never compromise! To do so is to surrender your values!" Now think about that. If you cannot compromise, you must then convince or coerce the other to do it your way. If that does not work, you make war on one another and ultimately you will have to kill the other!

How do you want to influence others? How can you influence differently than the current tactics? How will you influence with the vision you desire?

So how do you engage in radical politics? You take your sacred activism into every relationship. Reach out and befriend a woman who does not share your politics or religious views. Initiate conversations with those you know but usually do not talk about things that matter to you. Do this through genuine inquiry! Ask questions to understand. Don't debate. Ask them why they believe this or that. What about your beliefs frightens them? Can you agree to disagree without making the other wrong? What concerns do you share? Can you remain calm? Can you keep the conversation open? Allow your sacred activism —- the power of wisdom and love in action -- to guide you and create the change you desire. Deep listening and openness on your part will allow you to clarify, modify or strengthen your own beliefs. Our approach as women is often based on relationships with the other. Build relationships. Your composure, courage, and compassion will lead you to the right actions and invite other sacred activists to join you.

You may be having a conversation with a more conservative friend who denies that we can do anything about climate change, saying that we are seeing one of nature's natural cycles. You might calmly point out that we have the largest population ever in history. You believe that we do contribute to what nature is creating, and we can do our part to lessen human impact. We have nothing to lose and the avoidance of creating an uninhabitable earth to gain. What concerns them about our trying to lessen our impact? What exactly do they believe? If, rather than remaining silent, we calmly present what we know and believe and then listen to our friend's response, we may enter into a conversation that changes lives.

The Critical Issue of Climate Change

Your passion may be politics, gun control, the increase of violence, rape, drug abuse, or women's equal rights just to name a few. We often feel our issue is the saving grace for the world if we could only get people to see the need to agree with us. Does your Sacred Activism remediate the issue that undergirds all other issues--climate change?

Recently I was riveted by Josh Fox's film, *How to Let Go of the World and Love All the Things Climate Can't Change."* Fox travels the globe to follow the struggles of communities fighting the impacts of climate change. He articulates the facts with the soul of a poet about our profound connection to the earth. He speaks to indigenous people, and I was touched by their wisdom and depth of understanding. When the film ended, the issue of climate change went straight to my heart. Watching the film prompted me to evaluate my own feelings and beliefs on climate change. Whatever our passion, whatever our activism, we must weave in the relevancy of climate change, the giant container that undergirds all of our activist challenges.

Here's the bottom line. If ice is melting, water is rising, oceans are polluted, and we are heating up, there will be no other issues to work on. Even though climate change is highly controversial, it is the issue that could bring us all together. In unity we will stand for life.

I do believe in fact that women will have to take the lead here. For me women's rights, our influence, our perspectives are the thing that will make the world right. When we speak of violence, we must speak to how we are violating the earth. If we are speaking of rape, we must speak also of how we rape the earth. If politics is our focus, we must speak to the actions our government must take to forward action on climate change. Starting with our local government, our neighborhood, we must educate ourselves and others.

Climate change is the only issue that will matter and make a difference if we are to survive in the long run.

Find a way to watch Josh Fox's film. Invite your neighbors and friends. Talk about what you can do. Educate yourself and others on the solutions that exist now.

Ready For Sacred Activism? For Radical Politics?

Perhaps you don't feel ready to engage in radical politics. Perhaps the word "radical" causes you concern. You may also be uncomfortable with "sacred" and "activism." Or, alternatively, you may feel ready and eager to claim these labels. If you begin with personal work so that your spirit can come through, deepen your personal and spiritual development, and begin to take action, particularly political action, surrounded by love, you will be engaging in sacred activism and radical politics without any of the negative connotations or outcomes that these labels may imply. If any of the labels make you uncomfortable but you desire to make important change, set them aside. It's your actions that count, that will bring about the outcomes you desire, not any particular labels.

You've read my story. You've thought about the model for Sacred Activism that my actions and the actions of others have suggested to me. You've reflected on the implications for your own life. To end this journey that we have completed together, I ask you for three more reflections. They are particularly important to me, for only if your thinking has impact in your daily life will my book fulfill its goal of women waking the world. How will you move forward?

Self-Reflection #4: What Have I Discovered about Myself in Reading This Guide?

Reflect on the story of your life. Acknowledge any actions that you never gave yourself credit for.

What is mine to do to create the world I want to live in?

How will I integrate this knowledge into my daily practice?

RESOURCES

Books and Websites. All websites accessed May 2017.

Activating Peace Inside Out. http://activatingpeaceinside out.com.

Beak, Sera. http://serabeak.com.

BraveHeart Women Harmony Circles. https://www. facebook.com/BraveHeartWomenGlobalPurpose.

Caldicott, Helen Mary. 2017. http://www.helencaldicott. com/about/cv.

Dinan, Steven. 2016. *Sacred America, Sacred World: Fulfilling Our Mission in Service to All*. Newburyport, Massachusetts: Hampton Roads Publishing.

Dinan's book is a perfect complement to this book, taking activism to a global scale from many of the same premises I have introduced here.

Don, Meghan. 2016. *The New Divine Feminine*. Woodbury, Minnesota: Llewellyn Publications.

Eisler, Riane. 1987. *The Chalice and the Blade: Our History, Our Future*. San Francisco: Harper.

Evershed, Jane. http://www.imagekind.com/art/stunning/jane-evershed/painting/fine-art-prints

Feldt, Gloria. http://gloriafeldt.com.

5th World Conference on Women. (5WCW) http://5wcw.org.

Gbowee, Leymah. The Gbowee Peace Foundation USA. http://www.gboweepeaceusa.org.

Grey, Carol Hansen. http://carolhansengrey.com.

Harvey, Andrew. 2009. *The Hope: A Guide to Sacred Activism.* Carlsbad, CA: Hay House.

Herrick, Susie. 2017. *Aphrodite Emerges.* Woodacre, CA: Terdrom Press.

Houston, Jean. Author of 26 books. http://www.jeanhouston.com.

Katie, Byron. 2003 *Loving What Is: Four Questions That Can Change Your Life.* New York: Three Rivers Press.

Katie, Byron. *The Work of Byron Katie.* http://thework.com/en.

Kay, Katty and Claire Shipman. http://theconfidencecode.com.

Knapp, Mary. 2015. *Sacred Outrage: A Seasoned Woman's Guide to Soulful Citizen Action*. San Diego, California: Wisdom Moon.

Maathai, Wangari. Founder of the Green Belt Movement. http://www.greenbeltmovement.org/ wangari-maathai.

Maat, Tantra. 2013. *The Language of Creation: Your Original Design*. iUniverse.com.

Representation Project. http://therepresentationproject.org.

Shlain, Leonard. 1998. The Alphabet Versus the Goddess: The Conflict Between Word and Image. New York:Viking.

Shlain, Tiffany. 50/50. Video. http://www.letitripple.org/ films/50-50.

Simons, Nina. 2010. *Moonrise: The Power of Women Leading from the Heart*. South Paris, ME: Park Street Press.

Sister Joan Chittister. joanchittister.org.

Spretnak, Charlene. 2011. *Relational Reality: New Discoveries of Interrelatedness That Are Transforming the Modern World*. Topsham, ME: Green Horizon Books.

Stone, Merlin. 1976. *When God Was a Woman*. New York, NY: Barnes & Noble.

Tate, Rev. Karen. 2014. *Voices of the Sacred Feminine: Conversations to Re-Shape Our World*. Washington, D.C.: Changemakers Books.

Tate. Rev. Karen. Voices of the Sacred Internet Radio Show. http://www.karentate.com.

Werner, Erhard. http://www.wernererhard.com. Founder of EST. Erhard Seminar Training. Although EST has morphed into other names, this site is very informative.

Women Waking the World. http://womenwakingthe world.com.

Organizations Creating Change

Bioneers. http://www.bioneers.org. Bioneers is a fertile hub of social and scientific innovators with practical and visionary solutions for the world's most pressing environmental and social challenges.

The Charter for Compassion International (CCI). https://charterforcompassion.org. *CCI is a worldwide network that works to connect and nurture the heart of the global compassion movement. CCI fosters a peaceful world where all are treated with dignity, equity and respect and recognizes that everyone is born with the capacity for compassion. We envision a world in which all girls and women reach their fullest potential for global transformation, holding compassion as our driving force. We are individual women and in many cases are part of women's groups, women's networks and women's networks of networks who have all said, "Yes" to the concept of making "compassion a clear, luminous and dynamic force in our polarized world." We have the unprecedented and inalienable power to support, nurture, compliment, learn from, mentor and collaborate with one another. It's woven into the archetype of who we are as women.* https://charterforcompassion.org/women-and-girls-sector

Cultivating Women's Leadership Workshop. http://www.bioneers.org/every-womans-leadership/cwl-trainings. *Emphasis is placed on: practices for skill-building and leadership cultivation; strengthening both gender and racial justice lenses and analyses; making visible the legacy of imbalance reflected in our decision-making, organizations, and society at large; and connecting towards collaboration across cultural divides, siloes and differences.*

Foundation for Conscious Evolution. http://barbaramarxhubbard.com/conscious-evolution. *The ultimate goal of the Foundation for Conscious Evolution is the awakening of the spiritual, social, and scientific potential of humanity, in harmony with nature for the highest good of all life.*

Gather the Women Global Matrix™. (GTW). http://www.gatherthewomen.org. *GTW is a global sisterhood that connects women through circles. We create a safe place to share our true selves. Meeting in circle, we find our voices, claim our power, and celebrate our self-worth, leading to personal and planetary transformation.*

Indivisible Women of Nevada County. (IWNC) https://www.indivisiblewomen.org. *We are a results-oriented collective of women who are committed to engaging more fully at local, state and national levels to transform our political process. Resist, Persist, Inform, Reform. I cofounded IWNC in 2016.*

Institute For Sacred Activism. http://www.andrewharvey.net/sacred-activism. *The Institute For Sacred Activism$^{TM\,SM}$ consists of a one-year program with four intensives, offering a profound experience of what Sacred Activism can contribute to the inner and outer worlds, mystical practices for activists, and a deep grounding of the mystical journey as understood by major mystical traditions.*

Living Room Conversations. http://www.livingroomconversations.org. *Living Room Conversations are a simple way that anyone with an open mind can engage with their friends in a friendly yet meaningful conversation about topics we care about. These conversations increase understanding, reveal common ground and allow us to discuss possible solutions. No fancy event or skilled facilitator is needed. When people of all walks of life begin to care about one another, they can begin working together to solve the wicked problems of our time.*

Millionth Circle. http://www.millionthcircle.org. *"The millionth circle" refers to the circle whose formation tips the scales and shifts planetary consciousness. The phrase comes from Jean Shinoda Bolen's book* The Millionth Circle: How to Change Ourselves and the World, *which in turn was inspired by "the hundredth monkey," the story that sustained anti-nuclear activists in the 1970-1980s to continue on when conventional wisdom said that nothing (certainly not ordinary people) could deter the nuclear arms race between the superpowers.*

Shakti Rising. http://shaktirising.org. *We are a vibrant, eclectic community of individuals who recognize interconnectedness, believe in goodness, choose love first. Shakti Rising is a social change organization transforming the lives of women, girls, and the larger community. We cultivate the health and emerging leadership of women and girls, ultimately empowering them to utilize their personal transformation as a catalyst for positive change in their families and communities. This creates gradual cultural change that supports sustainable, cooperative, healthy societies.*

The Shift Network. http://m.theshiftnetwork.com. *The Shift Network is an organization with a big mission: To help humanity evolve and create a sustainable, healthy, peaceful and prosperous world. We are a transformative education company that partners with the top teachers, experts, and healers on the planet, across many diverse fields, to offer powerful experiences that support your growth and transformation — and the evolution of the collective. Through our events, courses, and media, we're committed to helping you create a conscious, meaningful life where you bring your greatest gifts forth in inspired action.*

Personal Clearing and Growth

Landmark Forum. http://www.landmarkworldwide.com
The Landmark Forum is designed to bring about positive, permanent shifts in the quality of your life—in just three days. These shifts are the direct cause for a new and unique kind of freedom and power—the freedom to be at ease and the power to be effective in the areas that matter most to you: the quality of your relationships, the confidence with which you live your life, your personal productivity, your experience of the difference you make, your enjoyment of life.

Avatar Course. https://theavatarcourse.com. *Avatar is a nine-day self-empowerment training delivered by a worldwide network of licensed Avatar Masters. According to many graduates, Avatar is the most powerful, purest self-development program available. It is a series of experiential exercises that enable you to rediscover your self and align your consciousness with what you want to achieve. You will experience your own unique insights and revelations.*

The SOCIAL ARTISTRY LEADERSHIP Self-Study Course. http://jeanhoustonfoundation.org/letter/self-study-course. *The Jean Houston Foundation promotes positive social change by developing international communities of leaders in Social Artistry™. People trained as social artists apply a wide range of cutting edge leadership and human potential development skills for finding innovative solutions to critical local and global issues.*

BIBLIOGRAPHY

All websites accessed May 2017.

Allen, James. 2017. *As a Man Thinketh*. http://james-allen. in1woord.nl/?text=as-a-man-thinketh.

Bioneers. 2017. http://www.bioneers.org.

Campbell, Kelsey L.. To Prove American Commitment to Women's Equality, Congress Should Ratify CEDAW. 06/18/2014. Updated 08/18/2014. http:// www.huffingtonpost.com/kelsey-l-campbell/to-prove-american-commitm_b_5505786.html.

Chittister, Sister Joan. Season 6 Episode 601. Aired on 03/01/2015 tv-14http://www.oprah.com/own-super-soul-sunday/what-sister-joan-chittister-believes-will-change-the-world-video#ixzz4ee8Rzb78.Cities for CEDAW. 2017. http://citiesforcedaw.org.

City & County of San Francisco: http://sfgov.org/dosw/ cities-cedaw.

Collins, Diane. 2011. *Do You Quantum Think?*: New Thinking That Will Rock Your World. New York: SelectBooks.

The Committee on the Elimination of Discrimination against Women (CEDAW). 2017. http://www.ohchr.org/en/hrbodies/cedaw/pages/cedawindex.aspx. Convention on the Elimination of All Forms of Discrimination against Women New York, 18 December 1979. http://www.ohchr.org/EN/ProfessionalInterest/Pages/CEDAW.aspx.

Dinan, Steven. 2016. *Sacred America, Sacred World: Fulfilling Our Mission in Service to All*. Newburyport, Massachusetts: Hampton Roads Publishing.

Emotional Intelligence. https://en.wikipedia.org/wiki/Emotional_intelligence.

EST – Erhard Seminar Training. http://www.wernererhard.com/est.html.

Evershed, Jane. 2009. *The Book of Jane*. Blurb. http://www.blurb.com/b/865006-the-book-of-jane.

Evershed, Jane. *The Book of Jane: The Story of Women*. Produced by Marilyn Nyborg. DVD/MP4.

Fair Housing Act of 1968. http://www.history.com/topics/black-history/fair-housing-act.

Feldt, Gloria. 2010. *No Excuses:_9 Ways Women Can Change How We Think about Power*. Berkeley, California: Seal.

50/50. http://www.letitripple.org/films/50-50.

Foundation for Global Community. http://www. globalcommunity.org/history.shtml.

Fox, Josh. 2016. *How to Let Go of the World and Love All The Things Climate Can't Change*. Film. http://www. howtoletgomovie.com.

The Free Dictionary. 2017. http://www.thefreedictionary. com/activism.

Gather the Women Global Matrix™. 2017. http://www. gatherthewomen.org.

Gelber, Steven M. and Martin L. Cook. *Saving the Earth: The History of a Middle-Class Millenarian Movement*. http://ark.cdlib.org/ark:/13030/ft1870045n.

Gerzena, John and Michael D'Antonio. 2013. *The Athena Doctrine: How Women (and the Men Who Think Like Them) Will Rule the Future*. San Francisco, CA: Jossey-Bass.

Global Community. http://www.globalcommunity.org/ fgcHistory.pdf.

Grey, Carol Hansen. *Gather the Women*. http:// carolhansengrey.com/seeds/gtw.html.

Grey, Carol Hansen. *2002 Feminine Face of Leadership Conference*. http://carolhansengrey.com/seeds/ffl. html.

Harvey, Andrew. http://www.andrewharvey.net/sacred-activism.

Indivisible Women. https://www.indivisiblewomen.org.

Kay, Katty and Claire Shipman. 2014. *The Confidence Code: The Science and Art of Self-Assurance---What Women Should Know.* New York: Harper Business.

King James Bible. https://www.kingjamesbibleonline.org/John-1-1.

King James Bible. https://www.kingjamesbibleonline.org/John-1-14.

Living Room Conversations. http://www.livingroom conversations.org.

McCloud, Shiloh Sophia. http://www.shilohsophia studios.com.

Newton-Small, Jay. 2013. "Women Are the Only Adults Left in Washington." http://swampland.time.com/2013/10/16/women-are-the-only-adults-left-in-washington. *Time*, October 16.

Politics. https://en.wikipedia.org/w/index.php?title=Politics&direction=next&oldid=603053878.

Rathbun, Harry J. *Creative Initiative: Guide to Fulfillment.* http://www.globalcommunity.org/cifbook/cifbook.pdf.

Thorwaldson. Jay. 2011. *On Deadline: Global Community disappears from Palo Alto*. Palo Alto Online. February 26. http://www.paloaltoonline.com/square/index.php?i=3&t=14505.

Spender, Dale. 1990. *Man Made Language*. New York: Pandora Press.

Sussman, Amanda. 2007 *The Art of the Possible: A Handbook for Political Activism*. Toronto, Canada: McClelland & Stewart.

United Nations 1975 World Conference on Women. http://www.5wwc.org/conference_background/1975_WCW.html

Ward, JoAnn Kamuf. 2016. *The Myth of Equality in the U.S. Workplace*. February 1. http://www.huffingtonpost.com/joann-kamuf/the-myth-of-equality-in-the-us-workplace_b_9103458.html.

Winchester, Simon. 2003. The Meaning of Everything: The Story of the Oxford English Dictionary. New York, NY: Oxford University Press.

UN Women. http://www.un.org/womenwatch/daw/cedaw.

Women to Women Building the Earth for the Children's Sake. http://traubman.igc.org/womantowoman.pdf.

ABOUT THE AUTHORS

Marilyn Nyborg, a successful business owner and high tech recruiter in Silicon Valley for 25 years, co-founder of Gather the Women Global Matrix and Indivisible Women, Founder of Gather the Women of Nevada County, Women Waking the World, is a master networker with 45 years of connections in women's leadership and women's circles. She is a Speaker and Tele-Seminar Leader, and Producer of a video The Book of Jane: The Story of Woman. Marilyn has taken her lifetime of experiences in Sacred Activism to develop an international network to restore feminine wisdom, values and influence in the service of all life. She is committed to a world that creates change in cultural values, personal choices, and policies worldwide that shift humanity's consciousness from separation and domination to integration and unity. Read more on womenwakingtheworld.com.

Marilyn Chambliss is a retired associate professor from the University of Maryland. She has two bachelor's degrees earned almost 20 years apart--one in Sociology and the other in Psychology. She also earned a PhD in Educational Psychology and spent her years at UMD studying the features of reading and writing that support communication between writers and readers. Her interests were sparked many years earlier by experiences teaching eighth grade English in a New York City Junior High school where students' reading skills differed markedly. Through the years, she became increasingly interested in what authors could do to facilitate a conversation with readers, even those who did not have strong reading skills. She has applied her understanding of writing that is good reading to this wonderful book. In the process, she has become a sacred activist herself!

Sushila Mertens has developed both left and right brain careers throughout her life. As a life-long learner with Master Degrees in both Education and Library and Information Science, she supported her family as a librarian; she also studied and applied the metaphysical and healing arts. She is passionate about education, personal transformation and empowerment. Sushila is currently a Reiki Master Teacher, Rapid Eye Technician, women's life coach, facilitator of circles, and sacred activist. Her life experiences have led her to conclude that empowering women to speak from their undistorted feminine and courage would enable women to lead in creating peace and cooperation on our planet. She applies her beliefs in working in local and state politics, Indivisible Women, Living Room Conversations, BraveHeart Women, and Activating Peace Inside Out. Read more on blinkandbreathe.com.

REACHING OUT TO THE MEN IN OUR LIVES

This book concludes with a final part to my story and what it taught me. Admittedly, this guide is directed toward women. But a recent interaction with a man from my past life of working in the business world brought my attention to our need to be sacred activists with the men in our lives as well. I start with the conversation between the two of us, followed by a letter directed toward the men in the lives of women who are sacred activists intent on moving forward.

The Conversation with a Former Colleague

We had not spoken for years. After catching up I asked his response to the recent 2016 election. He screamed, "I love him!" and proceeded to explain why. Finally he added that there is a war on white males. Wow, I thought. I believe many men may be falling victim to that idea. This was my response.

Dear Men Who May be Taken Aback by the Emerging Strengths of the Women in Your Life.

The women around you are rising, empowered, committed and leading. I know this is making many of you very unhappy. You feel we are taking your authority away. You conclude that we are competing for your jobs, emasculating you and abandoning you.

I've heard you asking, "What do you want? Don't you have equal rights?" I hope you can hear what I'm going to tell you.

For centuries you have been in control of power. It was only in 1920 that the women in the United States received the right to vote. And that's not been that long ago. You have written history often leaving us out. Only now are the contributions women have made over the years appearing in historical accounts. Your role as protector centuries ago evolved into a kind of ownership from which we are beginning to emerge. We need time to saturate ourselves in the divine feminine, where we can heal from wounds and where we can practice using our voice, our insights and our way of being free of your defining us and our roles.

It is important to us to know the feelings you are expressing. But the current experiences you are having have been our feelings and experiences for centuries. It would seem the pendulum has swung over to our side. The goal is that it comes to rest and be sustained in the middle. Please give us the time we need to strengthen ourselves, gain confidence and eliminate the internal voice of the patriarch. Our father's voice tells us "That's not ladylike" and more. Our mother's voice says, "Let Johnny win or go first." We need this time, and we need your love and support as we grow and adapt to our new model of womanhood that includes empowerment.

What do we want? We want to share power with you. We want an equal voice. We ask that you listen without interrupting. We ask that you refrain from claiming our ideas as your own. Stand behind us. Stand next to us. But it's our turn to practice leadership and influence outcomes.

Thank you all, our husbands, sons, brothers, father, uncles, and friends.

~Marilyn Nyborg

Contact Marilyn Rosenbrock Nyborg for mentoring or speaking engagements

marilyn@womenwakingtheworld.com
http://www.womenwakingtheworld.com

Facebook: Women Waking the world 2013

Printed in the United States
By Bookmasters